SYSTEMOLOGY
PILOTING

POCKET EDITION

Published from
Mardukite Borsippa HQ, San Luis Valley, Colorado
Mardukite Academy & Systemology Society
for spiritual or philosophical purposes only

SYSTEMOLOGY PILOTING

HOW TO HELP ONE ANOTHER

Advanced Training Supplement
developed by Joshua Free for
the Systemology Society

© 2024, JOSHUA FREE

ISBN : 978-1-961509-56-6

No part of this publication may be reproduced in any form or by any means, electronic or mechanical, including photocopying, recording, or any information storage or retrieval system, without permission from the publisher. This book is a spiritual artifact. It is not intended to diagnose medical conditions, substitute treatment or other professional advice.

This manual is restricted to students using:
The Systemology Professional Course -or-
The Advanced Training Course

Full use of this book also requires the
"Systemology Biofeedback" and
"Systemology Procedures
Advanced Training Supplements

Based on the lecture notes by Joshua Free for
the 2024 Spring Equinox release of the complete
Pathway-To-Ascension Professional Course and
Keys to the Kingdom Advanced Training Course.

First Edition Pocket Paperback — *March 2024*

mardukite.com

Take Systemology To The World!

The Official Mardukite Systemology "Piloting Manual" is now available to the public for the very first time.

Seekers working on the "Pathway to Ascension" using the Systemology "Professional Course" and "Advanced Training Course" can learn how to more effectively apply Systemology techniques to other Seekers and reach even higher levels of spiritual clearing.

This manual concisely organizes the most critical information necessary to expertly Co-Pilot another Seeker. The skills of Traditional Piloting are laid out clearly for all would-be Pilots to develop and then powerfully use.

Never before has Joshua Free so concisely explained the basic theory and practice of this spiritual technology. Master the art of defragmenting "energetic turbulence" and overcome the "spiritual implants" described in the Professional Course and A.T. materials, which keep us bound to this Universe!

The Pathway to Ascension Professional Course
#1 – *Increasing Awareness (Level-0)*
#2 – *Thought & Emotion (Level-0)*
#3 – *Clear Communication (Level-0)*
#4 – *Handling Humanity (Level-1)*
#5 – *Free Your Spirit (Level-2)*
#6 – *Escaping Spirit-Traps (Level-2)*
#7 – *Eliminating Barriers (Level-3)*
#8 – *Conquest of Illusion (Level-3)*
#9 – *Confronting the Past (Level-4)*
#10 – *Lifting the Veils (Level-4)*
#11 – *Spiritual Implants (Level-5)*
#12 – *Games and Universes (Level-5)*
#13 – *Spiritual Energy (Level-6)*
#14 – *Spiritual Machinery (Level-6)*
#15 – *The Arcs of Infinity (Level-6)*
#16 – *Alpha Thought (Level-6)*

Keys to the Kingdom Advanced Training
#1 – *The Secret of Universes (Level-7)*
#2 – *Games, Goals & Purposes (Level-7)*
#3 – *The Jewel of Knowledge (Level-7)*
#4 – *Implanted Universes (Level-7)*
#5 – *Entities & Fragments (Level-8)*
#6 – *Spiritual Perception (Level-8)*
#7 – *Mastering Ascension (Level-8)*
#8 – *Advancing Systemology (Level-8)*

Systemology Biofeedback
Systemology Procedures
Systemology Piloting

TABLET OF CONTENTS

INTRODUCTION TO THE MANUAL

- Introducing the Manual . . . 11
- Charting Flights on the Pathway . . . 13
- Taking Flight on the Pathway . . . 15
- Systematic Processing . . . 19
- Preventative Fundamentals . . . 22

SYSTEMOLOGY PILOTING:
THE MANUAL

- Traditional Piloting . . . 27
- Elements of Piloting . . . 32
- Piloting Seekers . . . 37
- Entry-Points to a Session . . . 40
- The Preliminary Interview . . . 43
- The Skills of Piloting . . . 47

APPENDIX

- The Formal Session (Script) . . . 59
- Basic Systemology Glossary . . . 66
- Additional Resources . . . 84

INTRODUCTION TO THE MANUAL

This manual is restricted to students using:
The Systemology Professional Course -or-
The Advanced Training Course

Full use of this manual requires:
"Systemology Biofeedback" and
"Systemology Procedures"

INTRODUCING THE SYSTEMOLOGY PILOTING MANUAL

Mardukite Systemology is a new evolution in Human understanding about the "systems" governing *Life, Reality,* the *Universe* and all *Existences.* It is also a *Spiritual Path* used to transcend the Human experience and reach *"Ascension."*

This advanced training supplement gives details for how to *apply* our spiritual technology to enhance personal progress on the *"Pathway" to Ascension* and also apply *Systemology* professionally *to others*.

This manual supplements our *Professional Course* series of lessons—available as individual booklets, or collected in two volumes titled *"The Pathway to Ascension"* The *Professional Course* follows after material given in the *Basic Course* booklets, or *"Fundamentals of Systemology"* volume.

The systematic methodology that we use to assist an individual to increase their *"Actualized Awareness"* (and reach gradually higher toward their *"Spiritual Ascension"*) is referred to as *"The Pathway"*—and that individual is called a *"Seeker."*

To receive the greatest benefit from this manual: it is expected that a *Seeker* will already be familiar with the fundamental concepts and terminology (previously relayed in the *Basic Course* and *Professional Course* lessons) of our *applied philosophy.*

As a *Seeker* increases their *Awareness* in this lifetime, their spiritual *"Knowingness"* also increases—which is to say their *certainty* on *Life*, on this and other *Universes*, and on *realizing Self* as an unlimited "spiritual being" *having* an enforced restrictive "human experience." A *Seeker* also *knowingly* increases their command and control of the "human experience." And this is a part of what is meant by *"Actualized Awareness."*

CHARTING FLIGHTS ON THE PATHWAY

Although there is a systematic structure to *fragmentation,* the personal journey experienced along the *Pathway* will be different for each *Seeker.* For example, certain areas will seem more *"turbulent"* or difficult for one *Seeker* than another. We tend to say that these areas have more *"charge"* on them—or that they are more *"heavily charged."* It is best to handle such areas when you are already feeling "good" and not in a situation (or condition) where that specific area is consistently being *"triggered"* or *"restimulated."*

As an applied philosophy, *Systemology* "theory" can be easily utilized in the "laboratory" of the "world-at-large" in everyday life. This is implied within the basic instruction of each lesson. Unlike other "sciences" that conduct experiments by making a change to some "objective variable" *out there* and waiting to see an effect, our focus is the individual (or *Observer*) themselves, and how *they* affect the *"Reality"* perceived.

Our philosophy is applied by using specific exercises and systematic techniques. These *"processes"* provide the most stable personal gain (and *realizations*) for each area; but only when actually applied with a *Seeker's* full *"presence"* and *Awareness*. Hundreds of such *processes* may be found in the *"Pathway to Ascension"* (*Professional Course*) material.

Applying a technique is called *"running a process."* *Processes* are designed with very simple instructions or *"command-lines."* To *run* a *processing command-line*, a *Seeker* may be assisted by the communication of that *line* from a *"Co-Pilot"* (as in *"Traditional Piloting"*). But even then, a *Seeker* must still personally "input" the *command* as *Self*. For this reason—and quite thankfully—*Solo-Processing* is possible.

TAKING FLIGHT ON THE PATHWAY

Processing Techniques are intended to treat the *Spiritual Being* or *Alpha-Spirit*; the individual themselves. The *"command-lines"* are *directed to* the individual themselves—not some *mental machinery* of theirs, and not even a *Biofeedback* metering device.

Systematic Processing is applied by the *Alpha-Spirit*—who then *Self-directs* command of their "Mind-System" or "body" (*genetic-vehicle*), both of which are "constructs" that the *Alpha-Spirit* (*Self*, or the "I-AM" *Awareness unit*) operates, but neither of which is actually *Self*. *Fragmentation* causes *Humans* to falsely identify *Self* as the "Mind" or even a "Body."

Some *processes* can be treated quite lightly at first; others may require a bit of working at in order to get *"running"* well. It is important to set aside a period of time when you can be dedicated to your studies and *processing*. This period of time is referred to as a *"processing session."* When a *process* does start *running* well, it is important to be able to complete it to a satisfactory *"end-point."*

Processing allows us to be able to *actually* "look" at *things* and even determine the *considerations* we have made—or attitudes we have decided—about *Reality* as a result of those experiences.

It doesn't do us much good to simply "glance"—or to *restimulate* something uncomfortable and then quickly *withdraw* from it once again, leaving more of our *attention* yet again behind and held fixedly on it.

Generally speaking, a *Seeker* continues to *run* a *process* so long as something is "happening"—which is to say, the *process* is still producing a change. Usually this is evident by the type of "answers" that a *command-line* prompts a *Seeker* to originate from the database of their own *MindSystem*.

Processing Command-Lines ("PCL") are not "magic words"; they do not "do" anything on their own. They systematically assist a *Seeker* to direct their own attention toward increasing *Awareness*.

A *Seeker* may also cease to generate new "data" from a *process* without reaching an *"ultimate" realization* as an *"end-point."* It is possible that additional "layers" (or even other "areas") require handling before anything "deeper" is accessible. If this is the case, end the *process*. But, if a *Seeker* is *withdrawing* from something uncomfortable that was incited or stirred up, then a *process* is *run* until they feel "good" about it.

One of the benefits to *Flying-Solo* on the *Pathway* is that the *processing* is entirely *Self-determined*. This naturally provides a certain built-in "safety" for a practitioner. Anything you *restimulate* by *Self-determinism* is *your thing*. It is not triggered or incited by some external *"other-determined"* influences (or other *"source-points"* in existence) that make you an *effect*. It can be more easily handled in *processing*—or you can simply let things "cool down" and come back to it again in another *session*.

While it may seem "mysterious" to beginners, a *Seeker* gets a sense for knowing how long to *run* a *process* only with practice.

Once you have spent some time actually applying material from *"The Pathway to Ascension" Professional Course*, there are many aspects of it that become "second nature" because they are, in fact, a part of our true original native nature. All we have done in *Systemology* is *"reverse engineer"* the routes of *creation* and *consideration* that are already *our own*.

SYSTEMATIC PROCESSING

Systematic Processing is primarily *looking* and *seeing "What Is"—As-It-Is*. "*Processing Command Lines*" (or "PCL") are really a query-line (or question) of "*what is*"? The response is based on whatever our *attention (Awareness)* is on, or directed to. Even when not worded as a literal question, a PCL is still a prompt for such a response. For example:

Q: *Recall a time when... (What is it?)*

A: *(It is) when such-and-such...*

Q: *Spot something in the... (What is it?)*

A: *(It is) that thing...*

Q: *Notice something about... (What is it?)*

A: *(It is) this...*

A *Seeker* is still permitted to *consider* or *wonder about* things. But to avoid having progress slow down to a halt during a *processing session*: the focus should be on what they *can identify*, *see*, or *know about*, rather than concentrating on "*unknowns.*"

To be effective, *systematic processing* is applied to only one thing/area at a time. It is for this reason that a *Pilot* must be aware of where a *Seeker's attention* is *fixed*—or a *Solo-Pilot* must be aware of it.

If *attention is* "stuck" on a point that can't be put aside, then it must be addressed first in *processing*, because that is the *fixed* point of *attention* that all other *processing* will take place from anyways. The "*presence*" that is elsewhere must be brought under *control* before other gains will be made "*in-session.*"

Defragmentation is a gradual process of relieving the "weight" off of the *Spirit*. This "weight" is mostly *persistently created entangled energy-masses*. A proper "*session*" should provide *some sense of release* to a *Seeker* for it to be effective.

If a *process* is not *run long enough*, there is a general feeling of "incompleteness." A *Seeker* may feel irritable as a result. Irritability and hopeless feelings are good indicators for a *process* being *"under-run."* The solution is to *run* the *process* longer.

The other side of this—*"over-run"*—tends to make things more *"solid"* or feel *"heavier."* Usually an area or target item was *defragmented* (a *release-point* was achieved) but since the *process* continues to target it as *being there*, it gets "pulled in" again, or else is *recreated*. This often happens when a beginner expects a single *process* to handle everything, or do it all, when it really requires applying many different *processes*, each providing another step forward as a fairly quick progression.

The *systematic* solution to an *"over-run" process* is to simply *"spot"* and *acknowledge* the point when the *"win"* or *"new realization"* had occurred (but was overlooked, not *acknowledged*, and *invalidated*).

PREVENTATIVE FUNDAMENTALS

If a *Seeker* has an *upset*, a *problem*, or any *attention* "stuck" on things they are worried about, it is not possible to progress in other areas until this handled. In the *Professional Course*, this handling is called "preventative fundamentals" because a *Pilot* must take care of these things first before attempting to spend *session* time in other areas. What we are *preventing* is an *invalidation* of our methods by a *Seeker* that is unable to apply *presence* of *attention in-session*. These fundamentals are treated in *Professional Course* materials:

1. A *break* or *upset* in the "*Flow-Factors*" — enforced or inhibited *communication*, *likingness* and/or *agreement*. [*Lesson-7*, "*Eliminating Barriers*"]

2. A "*Human Problem*" — present-time *attention* (*presence*) is occupied fixedly

elsewhere (and outside one's own control). [*Lesson-4, "Handling Humanity"*]

3. A *"Hold-Out"* — *attention* restimulated an area, usually because someone else *almost found out* about it. [*Lesson-6, "Escaping Spirit-Traps"*]

A *Solo-Pilot* looks over this list and determines if any of these factors are in play at the start of a *session*. In *Traditional Piloting*, a *GSR-Meter* may be used to *assess* if anything on the list *reads*. For example:

1. "Is there a *break* or *upset* of a *Flow-Factor?*"

[if it *"reads,"* check]

   a. "Is there a break in *Communication?*"

   b. "On *Likingness?*"

   c. "On *Agreement?*"

[then, *run* on which of *a*, *b*, or *c*, *"reads"*]

   a. "Was this ___ Enforced?"

   b. *"Inhibited?"*

In this first case: when you can *spot* the primary underlying source of the *upset*—such as *"inhibited communication"* or *"enforced agreement"*—there should be *some* feeling of *"relief."* If not: you may need to *reassess* the list.

The *"relief on spotting"* is either partial or total. If total: *acknowledge* it and continue on with the *session*. If partial: handle the *upset* (or *flow-break*) before continuing. It is handled by *spotting* the *flow* and *circuit*.

For example: did *you inhibit (or enforce) someone else's communication (&tc.)* or did *someone else inhibit yours?* Perhaps it was observing *someone else inhibiting another*. Whatever the case: *identify it*, then *spot* exactly what *communication* was *inhibited*. Then *spot* yourself in the situation; what you *did* and *decided* as a result of it, *&tc*. If the *turbulence* doesn't resolve or worsens: look for an earlier incident that was similar. If it gets more *solid*, it has been *overrun*: *spot* the *release-point* that was missed.

SYSTEMOLOGY PILOTING
(THE MANUAL)

> "MANY YEARS AGO, I REALIZED THAT 'THE WAY OUT' WOULD SYSTEMATICALLY RESEMBLE THE ROUTES BY WHICH WE ORIGINALLY DESCENDED."
> —*Joshua Free*
> *Backtrack Lectures*

TRADITIONAL PILOTING

This manual is a continuation of material presented in *"Systemology Procedures"* and *"Systemology Biofeedback."* Its emphasis is *how to "Pilot"* (or *"Co-Pilot"*) *Systemology* for traditional/professional applications. This is not a guide for *"what to process"* or *"what processing is"*—as such subjects are taken up in other manuals and lessons.

The purpose of this manual is to "pull together" all the data into an applied practice of *helping others—processing others.* There are *no* "special cases" in *Systemology*. We apply *New Standard Systemology* —given in *"Pathway to Ascension" Level-0 to 6*; and *"Keys to the Kingdom" Level-7 and 8*—from *bottom to the top*, to *all Seekers*. To deliver *processing-levels 0-to-6*, a *Pilot* must be *Level-7* or *8*, themselves. Only a *Pilot* that has completed *Level-8* is qualified to supervise paperwork for a *Solo Level-7*.

We originally developed *systematic processing* to train *Mardukite Ministers (of Zuism)* with skills to provide *spiritual advisement* or *counseling*. Initially, there was no prescribed *Pathway*. A *minister* studied our entire philosophy so they could apply the most relevant elements to handle the immediate concerns of an individual coming to them for assistance.

The first *"Professional Piloting Course"*—from 2020—is contained in the *"Metahuman Destinations"* volumes. It was there that the "seeds" of a *standardized Pathway* first began to grow; and the basic outline for a *"Formal Session"* began to emerge. It remains our basic *Pilot Training* material.

It is important to handle the immediate concerns of an individual before attempting to guide them along the *Pathway*. If the difficulties and upsets are not treated, then a *"hidden standard"* develops where *Systemology* is only considered to "work" *if* such-and-such a "condition" improves.

To effectively *process* another individual, a *Pilot* must apply *Systemology* with *certainty*—of the materials; of their own skill to communicate *processing command lines* (PCL); and their own ability to maintain control of the *systematic processing session.*

A *Pilot* develops their skill similar to how a *Seeker* ascends the *Pathway*; except in this case, the emphasis becomes applying the material to *someone else*, not just *Self.* For example: *Level-0* for the *Pathway* is *"communication." Level-0* for *Pilot Training* is also *"communication." Clear communication* is necessary for *all processing* to occur.

Piloting requires the *ability-to-confront* the *Seeker* existing across from you in *session*; just as the *Seeker* must be able to *recognize/confront* you as a *Pilot* for the *session.*

It requires an *ability-to-communicate* (project) PCL to a *Seeker* (clearly and directly with *intention*); and see that it has been received, or perceive the response; and then end the *communication-cycle* with an appropriate *acknowledgment*. [These are the same steps a *Seeker* practices on "objects" during *Level-8* (see *AT#7*).]

Traditional Piloting requires the same level of *presence-in-session* described in the *Professional Course* (PC) material of "*Pathway to Ascension.*" A *Seeker* has to have *reality* on the *session* for it to be effective. When you say "*recall a time you communicated...,*" does the *Seeker* properly receive, understand, and *process* the *command-line*? Does the *Seeker* even have any *reality* on *Life*; any *reality* on *communicating* at all? You will know by the *communication-lag*; the delay in getting a response or answer—and I mean an actual answer to the PCL; not just the production of a sound.

A *Pilot* must study *Systemology* to have any *reality* on it—otherwise, what are they delivering? If a *Pilot* hasn't gone through *processing* themselves, how are they to understand a *Seeker's* responses?

Traditional Piloting is not a "cultish" tactic; it cannot be enforced. It requires *two-way communication* with a willing *Seeker* that is interested in *Systemology* and their own case—or resolving the *Human Condition*. *Pilot Training* is as much about *communication* and *control* as it is about *processes* and techniques.

A *Pilot* must be able to skillfully deliver *systematic processing*:

—without *Evaluating* out loud to the *Seeker* about things that they should arrive at as their own *end-realizations*;

—without *Invalidating* with disbelief or suppression in any way, or trying to "correct" the data that a *Seeker* is giving; and

—without *Reacting* (or displaying any *emotion*) to anything a *Seeker* says or does during a *session*.

You don't say to a *Seeker*, "Oh, this is what is going on with you." We want the *Seeker* to realize the "*This is..*" part on their own.

ELEMENTS OF PILOTING

There are only four components to *Traditional Piloting*: the *Pilot*; a *Seeker* to *process*; the *session*, or *space* to have a *session*; and the *processing* or *processes*. That's all.

There is a big difference between *talking* and *being in-session* or *processing*. A *Seeker* needs to accept the *Pilot* as their "guide" (or as a *Co-Pilot*) if their presence is to be of any actual assistance to them. We start off, asking: *"Is it alright if I process you?"* And an initial line of communication is established. That's *Level-0*, or *square-one*.

We move on to the next requirement: and that is *presence-in-session*. Is the *Seeker's attention* somewhere other than the *session*? If it is, you aren't going to make any real progress. Whatever a *Seeker's attention* is *fixed* on is considered a *"problem"* to them —that's why they're *fixated* on it.

When a *Seeker* isn't able to apply *presence-in-session*, it is because they are treating something else as happening "now" in the *session*-space *and* time; even when it is not. You can even address this: *"Is this problem happening here in this room?"* or *"Is this person here in this room?"* You could even repeatedly alternate: *"Where is the problem?"* and *"Where are you now?"*

"Human Problems" is treated as *Level-1* on the *Pathway*; and it is *Level-1* for a *Pilot*. In this case, it is the matter of *presence-of-Awareness in-session* for *processing*. There is no progress—no *processing* taking place—if the *Seeker* isn't *present*. You aren't there to *communicate* with their *mental machinery*; you want to *process* a *Seeker*.

At the start of the *session*, you want to determine if a *Seeker's attention* is elsewhere; so you just ask: *"Is there anything that you are currently worried about?"* or *"Is there anything your attention is currently on?"*

New Standard Systemology is already designed for use by *Solo-Pilots*. Therefore, a *Professional Pilot* needs to demonstrate that they are of genuine benefit as an assistant to the *Seeker* on the *Pathway*. You aren't there just to read a book to them.

A *Pilot* ensures there is *presence-in-session* and a *communication-line* before *running* any other *processing*. Obviously, there are *techniques* and *processes* used to accomplish these basic points. But, for example, a *Pilot* isn't going to apply more "*subjective-styled processes*" regarding something that they can't visibly observe, unless they know the *Seeker* can receive PCL and follow commands regarding things that *can* be observed.

If a *Pilot* is having issues with getting a *Seeker* to focus *in-session*, or understand and follow-through with "picking up an object," don't start introverting the *Seeker* to *imagine/create* or *recall* things with any *reality*; because they don't have it (*reality*).

A *"condition"* is a set of circumstances encountered by *Life*—by the *Alpha-Spirit*—and in our work, we are predominantly concerned with the *"Human Condition"*; the *mental-circuitry* and *reality-agreements* associated with the *"Human Condition."*

When handling the *conditions* of *Life*, an individual has two choices: to *increase* or *decrease* their level of *Actualized Awareness*. An individually is either *knowingly direct* in *confronting reality "As-It-Is"* or they are operating *unknowingly, compulsively* and on *automatic*. As a route of *Self-improvement*—or when applied vocationally by a *minister*—*systematic processing* is only *piloted* (or *Co-Piloted*) to assist the *Seeker* in rehabilitating their own abilities.

The *Pathway* is marked by an increased *ability-to-confront*—leading to upper-level abilities of *"defragmentation-by-realization"* alone. It is also critical for a *Pilot* to be able to *confront/handle* the *processing-session*—and the *Seeker* within that *session*.

This means maintaining sufficient control over the *session* and *communication-line* until the *Seeker* can exercise true *Self-Honest* control of focused *attention* and their own *Self-Directed Actualized Awareness*.

Whether or not a *Seeker* is *Co-Piloted* up the *Pathway* through *processing level-6*, the upper-most levels are always handled "*Solo.*" This means at some point, a *Seeker* must take total responsibility for their own case. Records of this work can be reviewed by an experienced *Seeker*, but they act solely as an adviser to the *Seeker* in between *Solo-sessions*.

It is difficult for a *Seeker* to apply *presence-in-session*, or work their way along the *Pathway* (*processing-levels 0-to-6*), if they are currently concerned with "pain management" (especially chronic conditions).

Ideally, a *Seeker* becomes more able to *confront* past-*incidents* and is less likely to *compulsively* (*unknowingly*) create reactive *mental-images* and other *stored impressions* (possibly even at a cellular-level). [More details on this are given in the companion supplement, *"Systemology Procedures."*]

PILOTING SEEKERS

To apply the *Pathway* material for *Self-improvement*, a *Seeker* needs to feel safe in their environment; and free to *communicate* and *process* without inhibition. They can't be worried that the *"Pilot might find out something."* It is likely a *Seeker* is carrying around some bad experiences (which is to say *imprints*) concerning *communication* and *contact* with their *environment*.

It is up to a *Pilot* to provide reassurance. You might direct a *Seeker* to: *"Look around the room and spot things that are not being a threat"* or *"...not threatening you."* Ideally, the *Seeker* will also include *"The Pilot"* in their list of such observations.

Any technique that puts the *Seeker* in contact (*communication*) with their present environment is useful for achieving and maintaining *presence-in-session*, while at the same time, increasing *clear perception* and *Actualized Awareness.*

When a *Seeker* enters upon the *Pathway* from the *Human Condition*, they are *seeking* the *answer* to an ultimate "*WHY?*"— an ultimate "*Cause Of*"—and they are not going to be able to accept or understand the *answer*—the *Truth*—until it is fully and personally *recognized* and *realized* for what it is. And there certainly *are* answers when a *Seeker* is ready to receive them.

Even the degree to which a *Seeker*, themselves, is actually at *Cause*, is not likely to be accepted early on. Most elements that a *Seeker* believes to be their issue are misassigned or misidentified until they are able to realize their own true *Beingness*— being at *Cause*—and their participation in the *duplication* and *cross-copying* of *reality*.

This *realization* of *total responsibility* is a steep gradient to achieve—and it is not expected all-at-once. In fact, most of the background story of *this Universe* and the *Spiritual Timeline* (or *Backtrack*) of the *Alpha-Spirit* is not totally understood until the *upper-level A.T.* work. But it is *there now*, as the *"Keys to the Kingdom"* series of *advanced training manuals*. It is something we have not kept locked away from you.

Prior to *New Standard Systemology*, the common starting-point was *incident-running*—what we now treat as *"Confronting the Past"* in *PC Lesson-9* (*Level-4*). The first presentation of this appears in *"The Tablets of Destiny Revelation"* (*Liber-One*) as *"Route-1"* or *"Route-1R."* This had mixed results in the very beginning; since it required expert *Piloting* to apply, and there was no existing *Pilot Training* available.

We saw better results after publication of *"Crystal Clear: Handbook for Seekers"*—and it is still relevant with the *New Standard*.

If handled earlier on the *Pathway* then *Level-4*, *"confronting-the-past"* or *"incident-running"* (as a *counseling-action*) still requires expert *Piloting*. Even in this case, one can only expect to *destimulate* the area enough to treat with proper *processing* as a part of the greater *Pathway*. Sometimes too much is expected from the techniques early on; as if they are like a *"magic spell."*

Full or *Total Defragmentation* only occurs when the *Alpha Thought*—the *"postulates"* and *"considerations"*—associated with the *incident* (or *imprint*) is *realized* and *confronted "As-It-Is."* This ultimate level of *defragmentation* may not occur early on the *Pathway*—or if techniques are sporadically applied only as *"counseling-actions."*

ENTRY-POINTS TO A SESSION

The *entry-points* of any *case* are the same whether a *Pilot* is going to be able to take a *Seeker* all the way up the *Pathway* or not. Application of technique is the same.

A *Pilot/Co-Pilot* assists a *Seeker* in *accessing* the *incidents* on the *Backtrack*. The *Pilot* is not particularly interested in the *significances* of the *energetic-masses* and *terminals* entangled there. That is more of an interest to the *Seeker* themselves, about their own case. But a *Pilot* needs to be interested in a *Seeker's* case, and help maintain the interest and *attention* level of the *Seeker* on their own case.

The easiest way to get started, is with whatever a *Seeker's attention* is currently on. It is common, at the beginning of a session, to ask: *"Has anything happened that's been a problem to you?"* Or, if you are able to *Pilot* a *Seeker* for multiple *sessions*, you might modify this with *"Since your last session..."* and so forth. This creates *communication-lines* and gets *attention* off of *"human problems"*—*domestics*, *money* or whatever, by simply *acknowledging* it.

When using a *GSR-Meter* (as described in *"Systemology Biofeedback"*): if there is a *high-resistance* (*balance-point*) at the start of the *session*, some preliminary PCL may be required to lower the *resistance-reading*. Examples of this would be:

"Are you currently protesting something?"

"Has some condition gone on too long?"

"Has an achievement of yours not been acknowledged?"

"Are you having pains (body problems)?"

"Has something 'almost been found out'?"

"Is there something you can't tell anyone?"

Even if not prompted to disclose/speak the information to the *Co-Pilot*, often just the *realization* of *attention being on* these things is enough to bring down the *resistance-reading*. Of course, this may require *"repeated spotting"* of the data *"As-It-Is"* to get the *balance-point* into "normal range." Once it is: the *Pilot* starts each *session* by *running* the *"preventative fundamentals."*

THE PRELIMINARY INTERVIEW

Prior to any *processing*-regimen or standard *session*, the relationship between the *Pilot* and *Seeker* really begins with a *formal interview*. This allows the *Pilot* to get familiar with a *Seeker* and their *case*. But this is still best conducted in a *session-like* environment—and using a *GSR-Meter*.

The *Pilot* can ask the *Seeker* about times they've encountered trouble during their life—noting the *Meter-reads*, and the *area* or *terminal* that it *registers* on. This is only to determine the background and also to help steer what *areas/terminals* will require handling; but *processing* is not part of the *preliminary interview* itself.

The interview helps a *Pilot* "locate" areas with *fragmentary charge* prior to an actual *processing-session*; but also to gauge the *Seeker's attention* and *communication-lag*.

If a *Seeker* is experiencing *low-Awareness* states in-*session*—and/or they have no *reality* on any *recall-type processing* (*analytical recall*)—then focus on *"objective-style" processes* that involve *objects* and *masses* in their environment—even *points in space* if they can be worked up to it. This will provide a greater sense of *relief* for their present *state* than initially trying to go after the deeper sources of *turbulence*.

A key point of the interview is for a *Pilot* to get *reality* on a *Seeker's case*. You want to know what is the *Seeker's* ideal picture of *Life*, what is their existing situation, and how far of a departure is one from the other. By knowing this, we can bridge the gap in their *perceptions*—gradually separating the *Seeker's* "*Personal Universe*" from the "*Physical Universe*" in which it is entangled. A *true realization* of this *differentiation* is how one eventually "*Ascends.*"

There are many ways to engage in an interview—and a *Pilot* is likely to develop their own style for this as they gain more experience. You might simply say: *"Tell me about your life."*

One popular interview technique is often referred to as the *"Spheres Assessment."* In this practice: you simply go down the list of *Spheres of Existence*—and representative *terminals* for them—and note if there is a *Meter-read*, and/or there is noticeable *"charge"* based on the *Seeker's* observable reactions to each.

For the first *Sphere*, you have the *Body*, the *Human life*, their *name*, *&tc*. You move on to the second *Sphere*, concerning *"Home,"* and you have anything involving *domestic life*, or various *family-roles*, like *"mother"* or *"husband," &tc*. And you just keep going through all of the facets of existence in this manner. By noting the reactions to the various *areas* and *terminals*, a *Pilot* can apply *processing-levels 0-to-6* more effectively for a *Seeker*; targeting specific areas of *turbulence* that are holding them down.

A *Pilot* wants to pay particular attention to *Spheres* three (*groups*), seven (*spirits*) and eight (*divinity* and *religion*). You want to know what spiritual, mystical, social, philosophical, or religious groups and practices the *Seeker* has been involved with prior to *Systemology*. There is likely to be a lot of *imprinting* for these areas.

The obvious area to target is whatever a *Seeker* is most "upset" about (in present-time). Locate the *"can't do" justifications* or *considerations* attached to that.

Goals or *Purposes* are also heavily charged areas—which we treat more directly in *AT#2* and *PC-12*. But from the beginning, a *Pilot* should know what a *Seeker* wants to achieve in their life—their motivations and perceived purposes; but also *"failed goals"* and *"incomplete cycles-of-action."* By this, we mean, when they set out to do something, or intended something, but for whatever reason it didn't happen. It is likely some *Awareness* still remains on it.

THE SKILLS OF PILOTING

As said previously: *communication* is *level zero* for both the *Pathway* and *Pilot Training*. It is *step-one* of having a *session*. And it is key to everything else that we handle with our *Systemology*. Consider how far a *Seeker* could really get beyond *level-zero*, without the *ability* and *willingness* to *communicate* and *engage* on *any* subject; and without reactively *avoiding* what is *unpleasant* or *undesirable*.

Now, as we move into *Level-1*—"*handling problems*"—the first part, *communication*, already has to be in place; established. It is on such an incremental or gradual incline that we *ascend* the *Pathway*. Stable progress is built upon the foundations of previous stabilized progress. This is the only way that one can be sure of their own progress; and that nothing has been accepted blindly—or "*on faith*," as is said.

Most *session*-difficulties—whether *Solo* or *Co-Piloted*—generally stem from one of the *preventative fundamentals*. So, when in question, this should be checked periodically throughout a *session*, to make sure they don't require additional attention; or that something hasn't happened *in-session* (such as the *Pilot* making a mistake) that has put the *Seeker* out-of-session.

If a *Seeker* seems suddenly put-off by the *Pilot* or the *session*, the correct question to ask is: *"What have I done wrong?"* You do not ask *"if you did something wrong,"* because a *Seeker* is likely to just say *"no,"* or be dismissive. The *Seeker* may still indicate that you did nothing wrong; but by asking in this way, you also have a chance to check for any reaction on the *Meter*. It also gives them a better chance to volunteer information; because you *do* really want to know. A *Seeker* going *out-of-session* is easily missed; then you wonder why they aren't making further progress.

A *Pilot* needs to have an understanding of *two-way communication* and skill in its use. This is not only important for *processing*, but also for understanding the relay of information that occurs internally between systems; for example, following the *ZU-Line* from the *Alpha-Spirit* through *mental circuitry* and finally engaging with a *body*. All of these components are in *communication* with one another—usually *fragmented*, but it is still *communication*.

A *Pilot* should also understand the *Beta Awareness Scale*. This helps you determine what level a *Seeker* is *communicating from*. For example: an *enthusiastic* person is going to *communicate* far differently than an *angry* person, or a *bored* person, *&tc*. Not only do they relay *communication* differently in their speech and behaviors, but they also will receive *communication* differently. For example: a *sad* person is not going to respond very well to someone coming at them *enthusiastically hyper, &tc*.

The other frequently missed-point is the handling of a *presently perceived problem*. This cannot be overstated; because there is some strange expectancy that *Systemology* will still produce stable results even if one's conscious *attention* is *fixedly* elsewhere; and it won't. Of course there is a lot of *fragmented Awareness* that is still suspended elsewhere; but what chance have we of reclaiming *that* if we can't pull together what *attention-units* we currently *are* in a position to *knowingly control*?

A *Pilot* should observe where a *Seeker's attention* is *fixed* on something that they perceive to be still in need of "solving" or "controlling" — *stopping, changing, &tc.*

A bit of our *Awareness* remains on a line to those *terminals* and *areas* that we are considering *"problems,"* but of which are not actually present in our environment; only our personal or "mental" environment. And often, *"problems" are* generated compulsively and automatically by various *machinery, just* to *be* a *"problem"* for us —manufactured *just* to keep our *attention fixed on* all this nonsense; so we don't have a chance to figure out what is really going on. It's all been *systematically engineered* to operate that way; as becomes even more apparent in *upper-level* work.

A *Seeker* will get a handle on *"human problems"* after they get a certainty on being able to *create* them at will. Sounds a bit backwards, doesn't it; but it is truth. As long as an individual remains unable to *create* and *destroy* their own *machinery* and *circuitry,* they will remain *compulsively*—and often quite *unknowingly*—dependent on *programmed automation* to manufacture *reality* for them; based on long-forgotten and horribly *fragmentary reality-agreements* and *postulates*. In other words: they will remain ever *"at effect."*

Rather than *avoiding* areas, you want the *Seeker* to *"describe the problem."* You want to bring it into view, rather than having it linger perpetually on the periphery or side-view. Ask the *Seeker* if the problem seems *"farther away"* after each time they describe it. Our first goal here is to keep the solidity of *mental imagery* and entangled energy of the perceived problem from being right there up on the *Seeker* and overwhelming them. Because no real progress occurs that way. It has to be brought up—*resurfaced*—and treated *analytically*; not remain down in *low-Awareness* levels of misemotion and such.

Another critical component to *processing*, and too often missed, is the *acknowledgment*. This is how a *Pilot* "ends" one cycle of action, or communication, or in most cases, a single PCL. *"Thank You." "Okay." "Good."* It is an indication to the *Seeker* that their response has been received.

The *acknowledgment* is also important to keep the *Pilot* in check and following the standard procedures. Each PCL is given in its own unit of time and is a complete cycle of action. It isn't just one long string of commands.

Once a PCL is complete, the *Pilot acknowledges* its completion or response given. Then, when the *Pilot* speaks again, they are starting a *new* cycle-of-action or communication; they are *not* leading off of the *Seeker's* previous response. This is the only way to maintain *control* of a *session*. Let me tell you how to quickly lose *control* of a *session*. You ask a *Seeker*, "*How are you?*" And they say, "*Not well.*" And you say, "*Oh, how come?*" bzzzt—crash! You've just lost *control* of the *session*.

You've got to maintain *communication* without treating a *session* like two buddies having a good-ol' conversation. That is really not what *systematic processing* is. And you won't make any solid gains that way. You say "*Okay, thank you for telling me*" so they don't feel ignored. But if you keep letting a *fragmented Seeker* "steer the ship" than you aren't a very good *Pilot*.

The *acknowledgment* also ensures that a *Seeker's attention* does not remain *fixed* on any incomplete cycles-of-action due to the *session* itself. There are such things as *session repair-actions*; where a *Seeker* must essentially *repair* a *processing*-mistake that can occur whether *Solo* or *Co-Piloted*.

To *repair* a *processing-error*, a *Seeker* simply *"Spots"* the point where it occurred and then handles it properly. In the case of a *Piloting* error: the *Seeker* would *"Spot"* it and respond; and the *Pilot acknowledges* that response. For example: they *"Spot"* when you were shuffling papers around and it bothered them. You just say, *"Okay, thank you"* and *"is it alright with you if we continue the session?"* You're back in business. You don't need to get bogged down in blame. Just keep the *session* going.

The last point that I want to make — and it seems strange that we should need to point this out — but: *processing* is about the *Seeker*. The *Seeker* is the focus.

Going back to what is said about *sessions* not being a "simple conversation": there is sometimes a tendency for *Pilots* to do too much of the *talking*. Having studied the subject of *Systemology* more intensely, they generally know a great deal about what is happening with a *Seeker* that the *Seeker* hasn't fully *recognized* or *realized* yet for themselves. Don't deny your *Seekers* a chance to achieve these *realizations* for themselves; given them their *wins*.

But the point is: its the *Seeker's* time. This isn't a time for the *Pilot* to bring up their own case or editorialize the *Seeker's*. Your own stuff is for your *sessions*, when you are getting *processing*. Let's not have any of that *"Oh, yeah, this one time I..."* If you want to share stories of the *Backtrack*, save it for discussions that are not *in-session*.

The initial interview is also *two-way communication*—but the focus is still entirely on the *Seeker's* case; not yours. You don't want to be doing all the talking; that isn't going to make the *Seeker* get any better. You do enough *talking* to keep the *Seeker* engaged and attentive. Some good example questions to keep them *focused*, include:

"What are you interested in?"

"What activities do you enjoy?"

"What makes you happy?"

"What have you been successful at?"

"What do you feel you must do? —must not do?"

"Tell me about it."

"What do you think that is about?"

"How have you dealt with that?"

"Who else was involved?"

Whatever technique or application of our *Systemology* is handled by a *Pilot* or *Minister*, the stable results will only occur by handling the *Alpha-Thought*—the underlying continuously created or generated *postulates*, *considerations*, and *reality-agreements*, that are keeping the *Seeker's* attent-

ion-Awareness suspended on an *entangled fragmentary existence*, rather than actually *confronting reality* and treating it *"As-It-Is."* Once a *Seeker* has reached that point, a *Pilot* can step back and let the *Seeker fly!*

For the first time ever in history: we have the *Map*; we have the *spiritual technology*; and we have the *training* available. So, let's work together now, and start helping one another get out of this mess. Let's help one another reach *Ascension!*

APPENDIX: THE FORMAL SESSION

1. <u>BEGINNING THE SESSION</u>

"Would it be okay with you if we begin this session now?"

"Okay."

"Start of session."

2. <u>OPENING PROCEDURES</u>

　A. Presence In-Session

"Is there anything going on that might keep your attention from being present in-session?"

　(if *"no,"* acknowledge and go to *B.*; if *"yes,"* continue below)

"Okay. Tell me about it."

"Alright. How does that problem seem to you now?"

　(if *"further away"* or handled, acknowledge and go to *B.*; if *"closer"* or more turbulent, continue below)

"Spot something in the incident; Spot something in the room."

(this alternating command line is repeated as needed)

B. Orientation in Present Space-Time

"Get the sense of you making that body sit in that chair."

"Okay. Get a sense of the floor beneath your feet."

"Do you have that real good?"

(if *"no,"* acknowledge and repeat A.; if *"yes,"* continue below)

"Recall a time something seemed real to you."

"Tell me something you notice about it."

"Look around and spot something in the room."

"What do you notice about that?"

(these last four command lines are repeated in series as needed; acknowledge and continue below)

C. Control of Body and Mind In-Session

(two dissimilar objects—here given as *"Item-1"* and *"Item-2"*—are presented and placed within reach; or alternatively, at two distant points in the room, in which a command line for "walking" between them would be inserted)

"Pick up Item-1."

"Tell me about its weight."

"Tell me about its color."

"Tell me about its texture."

"Put it down."

"Pick up Item-2."

"Tell me about its weight."

"Tell me about its color."

"Tell me about its texture."

"Put it down."

(this series of command-lines may be repeated several times; when there is no communication-lag for several full series, and duplicate answers are reoccurring, acknowledge and continue below)

"Choose an object. Decide when you are going to reach for it. Then make that body pick it up."

"Now decide when you are going to put it down. Then make that body put it back where it was."

(repeat as needed; when there is no communication-lag for a full series of command lines, acknowledge and continue below)

"Close your eyes. Put all of your attention on the upper two back corners of the room and just get real interested in them for a while."

(if there are no visible signs of "strain" after two minutes, acknowledge and continue below)

D. Establishing the Session

"Do you have any goals for this session, or anything in particular you want to address?"

(acknowledge, then start a process)

3. STARTING A PROCESS

"I would like to start a process; would that be okay?"

"Alright. The command lines are ---. Does this make sense?"

(if *"no,"* clear up any misunderstood words; if *"yes,"* start the process)

4. CHANGING A PROCESS

(only the wording in a command line may be changed to make it more workable for a *Seeker*; to change processes altogether, the present process must reach an end-point)

Example: a Seeker expresses inability to "imagine" or visualize imagery.

"Okay. Well, just 'get a sense' of..." or *"Just 'get the idea' of..."*

Example: a Seeker expresses discomfort (or withdrawal from) recalling a particular incident.

"That's fine. What part of that incident 'could' you confront?"

5. STOPPING A PROCESS

(when an end-point has been reached on a repetitive-style process)

"We'll just run this process a couple more times if that's okay with you?"

(general process is run two more times)

"Okay. Is there anything you would like to tell me before we end this process?"

(**or**, if an end-point "realization" is communicated from a process)

"Alright. Very good."

(the formal end of a particular process requires a command-line)

"End of process."

6. ENDING THE SESSION

(once a process, or series of processes, is completed)

"Is there anything you would like to tell me before we end this session?"

(if *"yes,"* acknowledge and handle it with communication before ending the session; if *"no,"* continue below)

"Would it be okay if we ended this session now?"

"Okay."
"End of session."

BASIC SYSTEMOLOGY GLOSSARY

actualization : to make actual, not just potential; to bring into full solid Reality; to realize fully in *Awareness* as a "thing."

agreement (reality) : unanimity of opinion of what is "thought" to be known; an accepted arrangement of how things are; things we consider as "real" or as an "is" of "reality"; a consensus of what is real as made by standard-issue (common) participants; what an individual contributes to or accepts as "real"; in *Systemology*, a synonym for "*reality.*"

alpha : the first, primary, basic, superior or beginning of some form; in *Systemology*, referring to the state of existence operating on spiritual archetypes and postulates, will and intention "exterior" to the low-level condensation and solidarity of energy and matter as the 'physical universe' (*beta*).

alpha-spirit : a "spiritual" *Life*-form; the "true" *Self* or I-AM; the *individual*; the spiritual (*alpha*) *Self* that is animating the (*beta*) physical body or "*genetic vehicle*" using a continuous *Lifeline* of spiritual ("*ZU*") energy; an individual spiritual (*alpha*) entity possessing no physical mass or measurable waveform (motion) in the Physical Universe as itself, so it animates the (*beta*) physical body or "*genetic vehicle*" as a catalyst to experience *Self*-determined causality in effect within the *Physical Universe*; a singular unit or point of *Spiritual Awareness* that is *Aware* that it is *Aware*.

alpha thought : the highest spiritual *Self-determination* over creation and existence exercised by an Alpha-Spirit; the Alpha range of pure *Creative Ability* based on direct postulates and considerations of *Beingness*; spiritual qualities comparable to "thought" but originating in Alpha-existence, independently superior to a Mind-System.

ascension : actualized *Awareness* elevated to the point of true "spiritual existence" exterior to *beta existence*. An "Ascended Master" is one who has returned to an incarnation on Earth as an inherently *Enlightened One*, demonstrable in their words and actions; they have the ability to *Self-direct* the "Mind" and "Body" as *Self* (as a "Spirit"); and to maintain consciousness as a personal identity continuum with the same *Self-directed* control and communication of Will-Intention that is exercised, actualized and developed deliberately during one's present incarnation.

associative knowledge : significance or meaning of a facet or aspect assigned to (or considered to have) a direct relationship with another facet; to connect or relate ideas or facets of existence with one another; in traditional systems logic, an equivalency of significance or meaning between facets or sets that are grouped together, such as in *(a + b) + c = a + (b + c)*; in Systemology, erroneous associative knowledge is assignment of the same value to all facets or parts considered as related (even when they are not actually so), such as in *a = a, b = a, c = a* and so forth without distinction.

attention : active use of *Awareness* toward a specific aspect or thing; the act of "attending" with the presence of *Self*; a direction of focus or concentration of *Awareness* along a particular channel or conduit or toward a particular terminal node or communication termination point; the Self-directed concentration of personal energy as a combination of observation, thought-waves and consideration; focused application of *Self-Directed Awareness*.

awareness : the highest sense of-and-as *Self* in knowing and being as I-AM (the *Alpha-Spirit*); the extent of beingness directed as a viewpoint (POV) experienced by *Self* as *Knowingness*.

beta (awareness) : all consciousness activity ("*Awareness*") in the "Physical Universe" (KI, in *Zuism*) or else in *beta-existence*; *Awareness* within the range of the *genetic-body*, including material thoughts, emotional responses and physical motors; personal *Awareness* of physical energy and physical matter moving through physical space and experienced as "time"; the *Awareness* held by *Self* that is restricted to an organic *Lifeform* or "*genetic vehicle*" in which it experiences causality in *beta-existence*.

beta (existence) : all manifestation in the "Physical Universe" (KI, in *Zuism*); the conditions of *Awareness* for the *Alpha-spirit* (*Self*) as a physical organic *Lifeform* or "*genetic vehicle*" in which it experiences causality in the *Physical Universe*.

charge : to fill or furnish with a quality; to supply with energy; to lay a command upon; in *Systemology*—to imbue with intention; to overspread with emotion; personal energy stores and significances entwined as fragmentation in mental images, reactive-response encoding and intellectual (and/or) programmed beliefs.

channel : a specific stream, course, current, direction or route; to form or cut a groove or ridge or otherwise guide along a specific course; a direct path; an artificial aqueduct created to connect two water bodies or water or make travel possible.

circuit : a circular path or loop; a closed-path within a system that allows a flow; a pattern or action or wave movement that follows a specific route or potential path only; in *Systemology*, "*communication processing*" pertaining to a specific *flow* of energy or information along a channel; "*feedback loop.*"

communication : successful transmission of information, data, energy (&tc.) along a message line, with a reception of feedback; an energetic flow of intention to cause an effect (or duplication) at a distance; the personal energy moved or acted upon by will or else 'selective directed attention'; the 'messenger action' used to transmit and receive energy across a medium; also relay of energy, a message or signal—or even locating a personal POV (viewpoint) for the Self—along the *ZU-line*.

condense (condensation) : the transition of vapor to liquid; denoting a change in state to a more substantial or solid condition; leading to a more compact or solid form.

confront : to come around in front of; to be in the presence of; to stand in front of, or in the face of; to meet "face-to-face" or "face-up-to"; additionally, in *Systemology*, to fully tolerate or acceptably withstand an encounter with a particular manifestation without an automatic reactive response.

consideration : careful analytical reflection of all aspects; deliberation; determining the significance of a "thing" in relation to similarity or dissimilarity to other "things"; evaluation of facts and importance of certain facts; thorough examination of all aspects related to, or important for, making a decision; the analysis of consequences and estimation of significance when making decisions; also in *Systemology*, the *postulate* or *Alpha-Thought* that defines the state of *beingness* for what something "*is.*"

defragmentation : the *reparation* of wholeness; collecting all dispersed parts to reform an original whole; a process of removing "*fragmentation*" in data or knowledge to provide a clear understanding; applying techniques and processes that promote a *holistic* interconnected *alpha* state, favoring observational *Awareness* of continuity in all spiritual and physical systems; in *Systemology*, a "*Seeker*" achieving actualized "*Self-Honest Awareness*" is said to be in a basic state of *beta-defragmentation*, whereas *Alpha-defragmentation* is the rehabilitation of the *creative ability*, managing the *Spiritual Timeline* and the POV of *Self* as Alpha-Spirit (I-AM).

existence : the *state* or fact of *apparent manifestation*; the resulting combination of the Principles of Manifestation: consciousness, motion and substance; continued *survival*; that which independently exists.

exterior : outside of; on the outside; in *Systemology*, we mean specifically the POV of *Self* that is '*outside of*' the *Human Condition,* free of the physical and mental trappings of the Physical Universe; a metahuman range of consideration; see also '*Zu-Vision*'.

external : a force coming from outside; information received from outside sources; in *Systemology*, the objective '*Physical Universe*' existence, or *beta-existence*, that the Physical Body or *genetic vehicle* is essentially *anchored* to for its considerations of locational space-time as a dimension or POV.

fragmentation : breaking into parts and scattering the pieces; the *fractioning* of wholeness or the *fracture* of a holistic interconnected *alpha* state, favoring observational *Awareness* of perceived connectivity between parts; *discontinuity*; separation of a totality into parts; in *Systemology*, a person outside of *Self-Honesty* is said to be operating from a *fragmented* state.

flow : movement across (or through) a channel (or conduit); a direction of active energetic motion, typically distinguished as either an *in-flow*, *out-flow* or *cross-flow*.

genetic-vehicle : a physical *Life*-form; the physical (*beta*) body that is animated/controlled by the (*Alpha*) *Spirit* using a continuous *Spiritual Lifeline* (ZU); a physical (*beta*) organic receptacle and catalyst for the (*Alpha*) *Self* to operate "causes" and experience "effects" within the *Physical Universe*.

harmful-act : a counter-survival mode of behavior or action (esp. that causes harm to one of more *Spheres of Existence*)—or—an overtly aggressive (hostile and/or destructive) action against an individual or any other *Sphere of Existence*; in *Utilitarian Systemology*—a short-sighted (serves fewest/lowest *Spheres of Existence*) intentional overtly harmful action to resolve a perceived problem; a revision of the rule for standard *Utilitarianism* for Systemology to distinguish actions which provide the least benefit to the least number of *Spheres of Existence*, or else the greatest harm to the greatest number of *Spheres of Existence*; in *moral philosophy*—an action which can be experienced by few and/or which one would not be willing to experience for themselves (*theft, slander, rape, &tc*); an iniquity or iniquitous act.

hold-back : withheld communications (esp. actions) such as "*Hold-Outs*"; intentional (or automatic) withdrawal (as opposed to reach); Self-restraint (which may eventually be enforced or automated); not reaching, acting or expressing, when one should be; an ability that is now restrained (on automatic) due to inability to withhold it on Self-determinism alone.

hold-outs : in photography, the numerous snapshots/pictures withheld from the final display or professional presentation of the event; withheld communications; in Utilitarian Systemology—energetic withdrawal and communication breaks with a "*terminal*" and its *Sphere of Existence* as a result of a "*Harmful-Act*"; unspoken or undiscovered (hidden, covert) actions that an individual withholds communications of, fearing punishment or endangerment of *Self-preservation* (*First Sphere*); the act of hiding (or keeping hidden) the truth of a "*Harmful-Act*"; a refusal to communicate with a *Pilot*; also "*Hold-Back*."

holistic : the examination of interconnected systems as encompassing something greater than the *sum* of their "parts."

Human Condition : a standard default state of Human experience that is generally accepted to be the extent of its potential identity (*beingness*) —currently treated as *Homo Sapiens Sapiens,* but which is scheduled for replacement by *Homo Novus* (the "New Human").

imagination : ability to create *mental imagery* in one's Personal Universe at will and change or alter it as desired; the ability to create, change and dissolve mental images on command or as an act of will; to create a mental image or have associated imagery displayed (or "conjured") in the mind that may or may not be treated as real (or memory recall) and may or may not accurately duplicate objective reality; to employ *creative abilities* of the Spirit that are independent of reality agreements with beta-existence.

imprint : to strongly impress, stamp, mark (or outline) onto a softer 'impressible' substance; to mark with pressure onto a surface; in *Systemology*, used to indicate permanent Reality impressions marked by frequencies, energies or interactions experienced during periods of emotional distress, pain, unconsciousness, loss, enforcement, or something antagonistic to physical (personal) survival, all of which are are stored with other reactive response-mechanisms at lower-levels of *Awareness* as opposed to the active memory database and proactive processing center of the Mind; an experiential "memory-set" that may later resurface—be triggered or stimulated artificially—as Reality, of which similar responses will be engaged automatically; holographic-like imagery "stamped" onto consciousness as composed of energetic *facets* tied to the "snap-shot" of an experience.

imprinting incident : the first or original event

instance communicated and *emotionally encoded* onto an individual's "*Spiritual Timeline*" (recorded memory from all lifetimes), which formed a permanent impression that is later used to mechanistically treat future contact on that channel; the first or original occurrence of some particular *facet* or mental image related to a certain type of *encoded response*, such as pain and discomfort, losses and victimization, and even the acts that we have taken against others along the *Spiritual Timeline* of our existence that caused them to also be *Imprinted*.

intention : directed application of Will; to intend (have "in Mind") or signify (give "significance" to) for or toward a particular purpose; in *Systemology* (from the *Standard Model*)—the spiritual activity at WILL (5.0) directed by an *Alpha Spirit* (7.0); the application of WILL as "Cause" from a higher order of Alpha Thought and consideration (6.0).

interior : inside of; on the inside; in *Systemology*, we mean specifically the POV of *Self* that is fixed to the *'internal' Human Condition,* including the *Reactive Control Center* (RCC) and Mind-System or *Master Control Center* (MCC); within *beta-existence*.

internal : a force coming from inside; information received from inside sources; in *Systemology*, the objective experience of *beta-existence* associated with the Physical Body or *genetic vehicle* and its POV regarding sensation and perception; from inside the body; in the body.

invalidate : decrease the level or degree or *agreement* as Reality.

mental image : a subjectively experienced "picture" created and imagined into being by the Alpha-Spirit (or at lower levels, one of its automated mechanisms) that includes all perceptible *facets* of totally immersive scene, which may be forms originated by an individual, or a "facsimile-copy" ("snap-shot") of something seen or encountered; a duplication of wave-forms in one's Personal Universe as a "picture" that mirror an "external" Universe experience, such as an *Imprint*.

perception : internalized processing of data received by the *senses*; to become *Aware of* via the senses.

pilot : a professional steersman responsible for healthy functional operation of a ship toward a specific destination; in *Systemology*, an intensive trained individual qualified to specially apply *Systemology Processing* to assist other *Seekers* on the *Pathway*.

point-of-view (POV) : a point to view from; an opinion or attitude as expressed from a specific identity-phase; a specific standpoint or vantage-point; a definitive manner of consideration specific to an individual phase or identity; a place or position affording a specific view or vantage; circumstances and programming of an individual that is conducive to a particular response, consideration or belief-set (paradigm); a position (consideration) or place (location) that provides a specific view or perspective (subjective) on experience (of the objective).

postulate : to put forward as truth; to suggest or assume an existence *to be*; to state or affirm the existence of particular conditions; to provide a basis of reasoning and belief; a basic theory accepted as fact; in *Systemology*, Alpha-Thought —the top-most decisions or considerations made by the Alpha-Spirit regarding the "*is-ness*" (what things "are") about energy-matter and space-time.

presence : a quality of some thing (*energy/matter*) being "present" in space-time; personal orientation of *Self* as an *Awareness* (*POV*) located in present space-time (environment) and communicating with extant energy-matter.

processing command line (PCL) : a directed input; a specific command using highly selective language for *Systemology Processing*; a predetermined directive statement (cause) intended to focus concentrated attention (effect).

processing, systematic : the inner-workings or "through-put" result of systems; in *Systemology*, a method of applied spiritual technology used toward personal Self-Actualization; methods of selective directed attention, communicated language and associative imagery that increases personal control of the human condition.

realization : the clear perception of an understanding; a consideration or understanding on what is "actual"; to make "real" or give "reality" to so as to grant a property of "beingness" or "being as it is"; the state or instance of coming to an *Awareness*; in *Systemology*, "gnosis" or true knowledge achieved during *systematic processing*; achievement of a new (or higher) cognition, true knowledge or perception of Self; a consideration of reality or assignment of meaning.

responsibility : the *ability* to *respond*; the extent of mobilizing *power* and *understanding* an individual maintains as *Awareness* to enact *change*; the proactive ability to *Self-direct* and make decisions independent of an outside authority.

Seeker : an individual on the *Pathway to Self-Honesty*; a practitioner of *Mardukite Systemology* or *Systemology Processing*, that is working toward *Spiritual Ascension*.

Self-actualization : bringing the full potential of the Human spirit into Reality; expressing full capabilities and creativeness of the *Alpha-Spirit*.

Self-determinism : the freedom to act, clear of external control or influence; the personal control of Will to direct intention.

Self-honesty : the basic or original *alpha* state of *being* and *knowing*; clear and present total *Awareness* of-and-as *Self*, in its most basic and true proactive expression of itself as *Spirit* or *I-AM*—free of artificial attachments, perceptive filters and other emotionally-reactive or mentally-conditioned programming imposed on the human condition by the systematized physical world; the ability to experience existence without judgment.

spiritual timeline : a continuous stream of moment-to-moment *Mental Images* (or a record of experiences) that defines the "past" of a spiritual being (or *Alpha-Spirit*) and which includes impressions (*imprints, &tc.*) from all life-incarnations and significant spiritual events the being has encountered; in Systemology, also "*backtrack.*"

Spheres of Existence : a series of *eight* concentric circles, rings or spheres (each larger than the former) that is overlaid onto the Standard Model of Beta-Existence to demonstrate the dynamic systems of existence extending out from the POV of Self (often as a "body") at the *First Sphere*; these are given in the basic eightfold systems as: *Self, Home/Family, Groups, Humanity, Life on Earth, Physical Universe, Spiritual Universe* and *Infinity-Divinity.*

Systemology : a modern tradition of applied religious philosophy and spiritual technology based on *Arcane Tablets* (in combination with *"general systemology"* and *"games theory"*) developed in the New Age underground by Joshua Free in 2011 as an advanced futurist extension of the *Mardukite Research Org.*

terminal (node) : a point, end, or mass, on a line; a connection point for closing an electric circuit, such as a post on a battery terminating at each end of its own systematic function; a point of connectivity with other points; in systems, a contact point of interaction; a point of interaction with other points.

turbulence : a quality or state of distortion or disturbance that creates irregularity of a flow or pattern; the quality or state of aberration on a line (such as ragged edges) or the emotional "turbulent feelings" attached to a particular flow or terminal node; a violent, haphazard or disharmonious commotion (such as in the ebb of gusts and lulls of wind action).

validation : a reinforcement of agreements or considerations as being "real."

viewpoint : see *"point-of-view" (POV)*.

willingness : the state of conscious Self-determined ability and interest (directed attention) to *Be*, *Do* or *Have*; a Self-determined consideration to reach, face up to (*confront*) or manage some "mass" or energy; the extent to which an individual considers themselves able to participate, act or communicate along some line, to put attention or intention on the line, or to produce (create) an effect.

ZU : the ancient Sumerian cuneiform sign for the archaic verb—*"to know," "knowingness"* or *"awareness"*; in *Mardukite Zuism and Systemology*, the active energy/matter of the "Spiritual Universe" (AN) experienced as a *Lifeforce* or *consciousness* that imbues living forms extant in the "Physical Universe" (KI); *"Spiritual Life Energy"*; energy demonstrated by the WILL of an actualized *Alpha-Spirit* in the "Spiritual Universe" (AN), which impinges its *Awareness* into the Physical Universe (KI), animating/controlling *Life* for its experience of *beta-existence* along an individual Alpha-Spirit's personal *Identity-continuum*, called a *ZU-line*.

Zu-Line : a theoretical construct in *Mardukite Zuism and Systemology* demonstrating *Spiritual*

Life Energy (ZU) as a personal individual "continuum" of Awareness interacting with all Spheres of Existence on the Standard Model of Systemology; a spectrum of potential variations and interactions of a monistic continuum or singular *Spiritual Life Energy* demonstrated on the Standard Model; an energetic channel of potential POV and "locations" of Beingness, demonstrated in early Systemology materials as an individual Alpha-Spirit's personal *Identity- continuum*, potentially connecting *Awareness* of *Self* with "*Infinity*" simultaneous with all points considered in existence; a symbolic demonstration of the "*Life-line*" on which *Awareness (ZU)* extends from the direction of the "Spiritual Universe" (AN) in its true original *alpha state* through an entire possible range of activity resulting in its *beta state* and control of a *genetic-entity* occupying the *Physical Universe (KI)*.

Zu-Vision : the true and basic (*Alpha*) Point-of-View (perspective, POV) maintained by *Self* as *Alpha-Spirit* outside boundaries or considerations of the *Human Condition* and *exterior* to beta-existence reality agreements with the Physical Universe; a POV of Self *as* "a unit of Spiritual Awareness" that exists independent of a "body" and entrapment in a *Human Condition*; "spirit vision" in its truest sense.

AVAILABLE FROM THE **JOSHUA FREE** PUBLISHING IMPRINT

Collector's Edition Hardcover

THE FUNDAMENTALS OF
SYSTEMOLOGY

A Basic Course by
Joshua Free

*collecting material of six lesson-booklets
together in one volume!*

"Being More Than Human"

"Realities in Agreement"

"Windows To Experience"

"Ancient Systemology"

"A History of Systemology"

"Systemology Processing"

All *six* lesson-booklets of the first official *Basic Course* on Mardukite Systemology are combined together in *one volume* as *"Fundamentals of Systemology."*

Lesson booklets are also available individually!

AVAILABLE FROM THE **JOSHUA FREE** PUBLISHING IMPRINT

Collector's Edition Hardcover

THE PATHWAY TO
ASCENSION

The Official 2024 Systemology
Professional Course by
Joshua Free

All sixteen lessons available in two volumes!

"Increasing Awareness"

"Thought & Emotion"

"Clear Communication"

"Handling Humanity"

"Free Your Spirit"

"Escaping Spirit-Traps"

"Eliminating Barriers"

"Conquest of Illusion"

All *sixteen* lesson-booklets of the newest *Professional Course* on Mardukite Systemology are combined together in *two volumes* as *"The Pathway to Ascension."*

Lesson booklets are also available individually!

AVAILABLE FROM THE **JOSHUA FREE** PUBLISHING IMPRINT

Collector's Edition Hardcover

KEYS TO THE
KINGDOM

The Official Systemology
Advanced Training Course by
Joshua Free

All eight A.T. manuals available in two volumes!

"The Secret of Universes"

"Games, Goals and Purposes"

"The Jewel of Knowledge"

"Implanted Universes"

"Entities and Fragments"

"Spiritual Perception"

"Mastering Ascension"

"Advancing Systemology"

All *eight* A.T. manuals of the *New Standard Systemology Advanced Training Course* along with *three* training supplements are combined together in *two volumes* as *"Keys to the Kingdom."*

Manuals are also available as individual booklets!

Seekers and students of the *Basic Course* and *Professional Course* will also be interested in the *Systemology Core Research Series*. These eight volumes are a complete chronological record of the Mardukite New Thought developments from the Systemology Society, published in 2019 through 2023.

The *Systemology Core* begins with the first professional publication released when the *Mardukite Systemology Society* emerged from the underground in 2019, with: *"The Tablets of Destiny Revelation."*

The Tablets of Destiny Revelation:
*How Long-Lost Anunnaki Wisdom
Can Change the Fate of Humanity*

Crystal Clear: *Handbook for Seekers*

Metahuman Destinations (2 *volumes*)

Imaginomicon:
Approaching Gateways to Higher Universes

Way of the Wizard: *Utilitarian Systemology*

Systemology-180: *Fast-Track to Ascension*

Systemology Backtrack:
Reclaiming Spiritual Power & Past-Life Memory

PUBLISHED BY THE **JOSHUA FREE** IMPRINT REPRESENTING

The Mardukite Academy of Systemology

mardukite.com

www.ingramcontent.com/pod-product-compliance
Lightning Source LLC
LaVergne TN
LVHW012125070526
838202LV00056B/5853